Wild Britain

Sea Cliffs

Louise and Richard Spilsbury

Heinemann
LIBRARY

www.heinemann.co.uk
Visit our website to find out more information about Heinemann Library books.

To order:
☎ Phone 44 (0) 1865 888066
▤ Send a fax to 44 (0) 1865 314091
▢ Visit the Heinemann Bookshop at www.heinemann.co.uk to browse our catalogue and order online.

First published in Great Britain by Heinemann Library, Halley Court, Jordan Hill, Oxford OX2 8EJ, part of Harcourt Education Ltd. Heinemann is a registered trademark of Harcourt Education Ltd.

Editorial: Lucy Thunder and Helen Cox
Design: David Poole and Celia Floyd
Illustrations: Alan Fraser and Geoff Ward
Picture Research: Catherine Bevan and Peter Morris
Production: Sevy Ribierre

Originated by Dot Gradations
Printed and bound in Hong Kong, China by South China Printing

ISBN 0 431 03920 8
07 06 05 04 03
10 9 8 7 6 5 4 3 2 1

British Library Cataloguing in Publication Data
Spilsbury, Louise and Spilsbury, Richard
Sea cliffs. – (Wild Britain)
577.5'1'0941
A full catalogue record for this book is available from the British Library.

Acknowledgements

The Publishers would like to thank the following for permission to reproduce photographs: Bryan and Cherry Alexander p25; Bruce Coleman pp4 (Ron Lilley), 5 (Iain Sarjeant), 12 (Colin Varndell), 14 (Sir Jeremy Grayson), 15 (Derek Croucher), 26 (Andrew Purcell); Corbis pp7 (Annie Poole), 8 (Sally A Morgan), 11 (Kevin Schafer), 13 (Adam Woolfitt); Ecoscene pp28 (Andrew Brown), 29 (Leaper); FLPA pp10, 22 (S Jonasson), 16 (Peggy Heard), 17 (Chris Newton), 18 (G E Hyde) 19 (A J Roberts), 20 (Philip Perry), 21 (J Watkins), 27 (A R Hamblin); GSF Picture Library pp6, 23; Nature Picture Library p24; NHPA p9 (E A Janes).

Cover photograph of Marine Drive, near Douglas, Isle of Man, reproduced with permission of Bruce Coleman Collection (Derek Croucher).

The publishers would like to thank Michael Scott for his assistance in the preparation of this book.

Every effort has been made to contact copyright holders of any material reproduced in this book. Any omissions will be rectified in subsequent printings if notice is given to the Publisher.

Contents

Any words appearing in the text in bold, **like this**, are explained in the Glossary.

What is a sea cliff?

These cliffs are in East Sussex. They are called the Seven Sisters cliffs.

There are cliffs all around the coast of Britain. A sea cliff is a very steep face of rock where the land meets the sea.

Many plants and animals live on sea cliffs, like these in Scotland.

A **habitat** is the natural home of a group of plants and animals. In this book we look at some of the plants and animals that live, grow and **reproduce** in a cliff habitat.

5

Types of cliff

The soft rock on this cliff crumbles easily. Few plants and animals can live here.

Some cliffs are made from soft rock. When the wind, rain and sea batter them, the surface crumbles away. It is hard for many plants or animals to live here.

The ledges on a cliff made from hard rock last a long time.
Gulls fly in from the sea to rest on these ledges.

Cliffs made from harder rock are also shaped
by the wind and rain, but much more
slowly. Ledges form where rock falls away.
Plants can grow on these ledges and sea
birds can land on them.

Changes

These cliff-top flowering plants are called pink thrift.

In spring and summer, flowers grow on cliff tops. **Insects** visit the flowers to drink their **nectar**. Sea birds make **nests** on cliffs to lay their **eggs** in.

The cliff is a much quieter place in winter. Many birds have flown away and the flowers have died.

In autumn and winter the cliffs are less colourful because there are few flowers. Many sea birds have flown out to sea to live. Some have **migrated** to other places.

Living there

Only birds, like these guillemots, can rest on a steep cliff face. Birds have wings to fly there.

The side of a cliff is called the cliff face. The cliff face is steep and it is difficult for plants and animals to hold on safely.

Some sheep **graze** on cliff tops.

The flatter land at the top of the cliff is called the cliff top. There is **soil** here, so plants can grow. Rabbits, moles and other animals live here. They **shelter** among the plants or in the ground.

Plants on top

A gorse bush has spiky **stems**. The gorse spikes stop animals like sheep and rabbits from eating it.

Life is hard for plants on a cliff top. There is only a thin layer of **soil** on the rock. Tough hawthorn trees and gorse bushes are the main big plants here.

The pink plants in this picture are heathers, and those with golden flowers are gorse.

Many cliff-top plants grow close to the ground to keep out of the wind. Grasses, heather, thistles and rock rose are some low-growing plants on a cliff top.

Plants on the cliff face

These patches of orange and brown are different kinds of lichen. Lichen grows on bare rock.

Lichen grows on the cliff face. When a patch of lichen dies it mixes with bits of crumbling rock and becomes soil. Moss and other small plants grow in this **soil**.

Thrift forms clumps of pink flowers which are shaped like a cushion.

Small plants on the cliff face often grow in rock cracks. The rock **shelters** the plants from the wind. Plants like thrift and sea campion can grow here.

Cliff-top insects

The hawthorn shield bug is the same colour as a hawthorn leaf. This hides the bug from birds that want to eat it.

Some cliff-top **insects** eat parts of plants. Grasshoppers and crickets feed on grasses. Hawthorn shield bugs eat the leaves and fruit of the hawthorn tree.

The devil's coach horse beetle moves quickly across the ground to catch food.

Some beetles that live on cliffs eat other insects. The devil's coach horse beetle grows to about 3 centimetres long. It catches and eats other insects.

Butterflies and moths

This is the caterpillar of the common blue butterfly.

In spring, some butterflies and moths lay their **eggs** on cliff-top plants. When the **caterpillars** come out of the eggs they eat the plant leaves.

This six-spot burnet moth is drinking nectar. Its bright colours warn birds that it tastes bad so they do not eat it.

Adult butterflies and moths mostly feed on sweet **nectar** from flowers. They suck it up using a long tongue called a proboscis.

Birds at the cliff top

This Manx shearwater is sitting outside the entrance to her nest hole.

Sea birds spend most of their lives at sea. They only come to land to **reproduce**. **Female** Manx shearwaters lay their eggs in old rabbit holes on grassy cliff tops.

Puffin parents carry fish in their beaks back to their young.

Some puffins dig out a nest hole with their beak and feet. They make a soft bed of feathers and grass at the back of the hole. The female lays one egg. When the chick comes out, its parents feed it fish.

Birds on the cliff face

This guillemot's egg is pear-shaped so that it does not roll off the rocky ledge.

Some sea birds lay their **eggs** on the cliff face. The **female** guillemot does not make a **nest**. She lays a single pear-shaped egg on a rocky ledge.

Gannets cover their eggs with their feet to keep them warm.

Gannets make nests of seaweed and grass.
The chicks come out of the eggs after
about 40 days. The parent birds catch fish
to feed the young.

Hunters of the cliff

Peregrines fly high in the sky. They catch birds, like puffins or kittiwakes, to eat.

Some birds hunt other animals for food. Peregrines, kestrels and sea eagles fly over cliffs. They hunt for young sea birds and small **mammals**, like mice, to eat.

The Arctic skua hunts like a pirate over the sea. It chases other birds and steals food that they have caught.

The Arctic skua chases puffins or guillemots that are carrying fish back to their chicks. The skua chases them until they drop the fish. Then it gobbles up the stolen food.

Cliff-top mammals

This field vole eats grass leaves and **stems**. It always uses the same paths through the grass.

Mammals like rabbits, voles, moles and rats live near the edge of the cliff top. They live in holes underground. Foxes and badgers live further back from the edge.

Rabbits come out of their holes to eat grass. When a hungry sea bird comes near, they dive into their holes to hide.

Large sea birds, like great black-backed gulls, hunt rabbits. Rabbits warn each other about sea birds coming by thumping their back feet on the ground.

Dangers

Lots of people enjoy walking on cliff tops. They should keep to the paths.

Walkers can disturb animals on the cliff top.
It is important that walkers keep to the paths.
They should also keep dogs on a lead if they
are walking past animals such as sheep.

People who drop rubbish are selfish. They spoil the cliffs for the animals living there and for other people.

If people drop rubbish on cliff tops, they spoil these places for everyone. Some animals die from rubbish that people have dropped. They can get stuck inside old cans or bottles.

Food chain

All plants and animals in a cliff **habitat** are connected through the food they eat. Food chains show how different living things are linked. Here is one example:

The peregrine eats the vole.

The vole eats the grass.

The artwork on this page is not to scale.

Glossary

caterpillar caterpillars hatch out of eggs and become adult butterflies or moths

egg shell that some baby animals grow inside before they come out

female animal that can lay eggs or give birth to live young. A female human is a girl or a woman.

graze to eat growing grass

habitat natural home of a group of plants and animals

insect small animal that has six legs when an adult

mammals group of animals that feed their babies on milk. They have hair on their bodies.

migrate when animals move to a warmer place for the winter

nectar sweet, sugary juice in the centre of a flower

nest something an animal makes to rest in or to have young in

reproduce when plants and animals make young just like themselves

roots parts of a plant that grow in the soil. They take in water and food.

shelter somewhere safe to stay, live and have young

soil also called mud or earth. Soil is made up of lots of different things, including tiny bits of rock and dead plants.

stem the stalk that holds up the leaves and flowers of a plant

Index